AM I GOD'S WILL?

"It's Tough Being a Biracial Child!"

AM I GOD'S WILL?

"It's Tough Being a Biracial Child!"

Taniyah Nicole Eyer

CAMDEN COURT PUBLISHERS, INC.

SALT LAKE CITY, UTAH

CAMDEN COURT PUBLISHERS, INC.
9160 South 300 West, Suite 2
Sandy, UT 84070

AM I GOD'S WILL?
Copyright © 1996 Taniyah Nicole Eyer
All rights reserved.

PRINTING HISTORY
First Printing May 1997

ISBN 1-890828-03-3

PRINTED IN THE UNITED STATES OF AMERICA
10 9 8 7 6 5 4 3 2 1

To my mom and dad.

Dedicated to the memories of someone *very*, *very* special:
Bradford Scott Bills

ACKNOWLEDGMENTS

Special thanks to: Klaus Kelterborn, Nana the Younger (Marylyn Eyer), Nana the Elder (Margaret Brothers), my cousins Elaine and David Davis, Grandma Anna Parks, Grandma and Grandpa Strong (John & Analee), Mrs Marston and my classmates at Logos School; Mrs. Leishman, Mr. Stevenson, my classmates in Utah; my teachers and classmates at Minnehaha Academy: Mrs. Styrlund, Mr. Hauge, Mrs. Higginbotham, Mr. Olson, Mr. Borner, especially Allison Heille; Peggy Roland, Tressie Johnson, Katja Buschnyj, Bishop Kacher, Barbara and Stan Cox, Glen Roundy, Nyron and Elaine Sorenson, Chelsey and Ashly Barlocker, Arlene and Tom Miller, Grandma Thompson, Tiffany Rex, the Pages, Jan and Cliff Spendlove, Aunt Lil and Norman Johnson, Curtis Leslie and family, Travis and Chellise Thurston, Robbie and Jeff Brown, Wendy Draper, Whitney Syphus, Tina Prior, Michael and David Wood, Christy Hinton, Whitney Bland, and finally, my very best friend, Tailona Johnson. Thank you for accepting me *unconditionally!*

Matthew 25:40

Thank you, Laurelle Dalton, for the many hours you spent working on the illustrations for my story.

A Little Child

A little child am I
With cheerful brown eyes
that sometimes are made sad and cries.
What race am I you ask?
Why do you insist on making that a task?
A little child am I
A little child who prays at night,
that people will stop seeing me as
black or white.
A little child whom all must see,
is simply happy being me.
A little child am I
loving life beneath God's big, blue sky.
Come, take my hand and see,
If there's a difference between
you and me
—Taniyah Nicole Eyer

INTRODUCTION

Hi, my name is Taniyah Nicole Eyer. I am ten years old and judging by my name, you probably would not know I am biracial. If your were to see me without my parents, you would probably still not know. I probably would have never known either if people hadn't started making me aware that I was biracial.

It's strange how people have a way of taking a kid's happy world and turning it upside down. Take me for instance. One day I was just a normal kid going to school and doing all the things a good student is supposed to do but before the day was over, a few hurtful and confusing words had changed my carefree and "normal" life. This is how it happened.

I : THE BOY

The school bell sounded and I quickly gathered my books to go meet my mom. I wanted her to know I had been chosen to be the narrator for the school's Christmas program. Smiling over the news, I rushed to get outside. I had barely stepped out into the fresh December air when I heard someone call my name.

I stopped, looked back toward the crowded doorway, and tried to find the person who had said it. Unable to, I turned and continued across the schoolyard toward our car, where my mom sat patiently waiting for me.

Suddenly, I heard my name being called out again, except this time I didn't bother to look around. I figured if someone was trying to get my attention, they'd either catch up with me or talk to me tomorrow. I was anxious to share my exciting news with my mom.

A boy from my class suddenly ran in front of me, blocking my path.

"I was calling you, Taniyah," he said, sounding a bit annoyed.

"Oh, that was you?" I inquired.

"Yes," he replied.

"Sorry," I apologized. "I wasn't ignoring you. I did hear my name being called, but I didn't know who it was or where it came from."

He didn't say anything.

"Well, why did you call me?" I asked him.

"I want to ask you a question; can I?" he said, looking at the ground instead of me.

"I guess so," I told him.

He looked up at me with a weird look on his face but didn't say anything.

"Well, what's your question?" I asked him.

He hesitated. "Are you sure you won't get mad at me if I ask it?" He asked with a frown on his face, still looking at me rather strangely—or scared.

"No," I said as I started wondering what dumb thing he wanted to ask that might make me get angry.

"Are you really sure you won't get mad?" he asked again.

"Look, my mom's waiting. Ask your question!" I snapped. "I told you I won't get mad. Anyway, Mom says only dogs get mad; people get angry."

I think he could see that I was becoming angry, although I was really getting scared wondering what he was going to ask. He finally asked his question.

"Is it hard on you?" he asked with that weird look and frown on his face.

"Is *what* hard on me?" I asked, not knowing what he was talking about.

"Being half-black and half-white?" he asked nervously while staring at the ground.

"What do you mean? I'm not a zebra," I said, growing upset with him.

"No, Taniyah, that's not what I meant," he quickly replied. "I mean, having a white dad and a *black* mom?"

I folded my arms and stared at him without saying a word. His question had bothered me, especially the way he had said "black" when referring to my mom. *What was wrong with my mom being black?* I felt my eyes watering and bit down hard on my lips.

"You said I could ask you, and that you wouldn't get

mad," he said rather quietly.

"I am not a dog!" I snapped at him.

"I mean *angry*," he said. "And, Taniyah, I wasn't calling you a dog. I always say mad."

I could see he wasn't trying to be mean yet his question had given me a funny feeling inside. I had never thought about my color. I looked at one of my hands and then at him. I didn't know what to say. I honestly didn't know how it felt being half-black and half-white. Trying hard not to cry, I told him I hadn't really thought about it and asked if I could answer his question the next day.

"Sure." He shrugged his shoulders and stepped from in front of me.

I had barely started leaving when he again called out my name. I debated whether to acknowledge that I had heard him. I finally turned and looked at him though I didn't want to.

"Thanks, Taniyah. And I'm glad you got the part of narrator—you'll be awesome," he said, smiling.

I nodded my head and then turned to go meet my mom. My news didn't seem so exciting anymore.

• • •

At dinner I sat thinking about what the boy had asked me. Mom noticed how quiet I was and asked if something was bothering me. I told her a boy had asked me a question and I was thinking about it. She wanted to know what but I told her I would tell her after I gave it some thought and had an answer. She asked if she might be able to help me with it. I told her I didn't think so. I saw a disappointed look come to her face, especially in her eyes, and felt sad that I could not share his question with her. I don't often think about things without first asking my mom's opinion, but this time I knew I had to think about things and come up with how I felt and not mom. After all, the boy had not asked me how she felt, but how *I* felt.

"Mom, just trust me for now," I said, smiling at her. "I will tell you what he asked but I need to think about his question and try to come up with my own answer first." She smiled and nodded her head, but I knew not knowing was disturbing her.

• • •

After dinner I went to my room and sat at my desk thinking about the boy's question. I thought about my life and wondered how being a half-black and half-white kid felt. Remembering how Mom says it helps to write down both sides when trying to decide something, I started jotting down how I felt. By the time Mom told me it was time to get ready for bed, I had finished jotting down the things that had happened to me so far and how they had affected my life.

After brushing my teeth, I stood looking at myself for a long time in the mirror. Staring back at me was *me*—the same me that always did, except now I stared at someone the boy had said was half-black and half-white. I put my hand in the middle of the front of my face and tried to determine which half was white and which half was black. I couldn't. All that stared back at me was one solid color.

I got into bed but could not sleep. *Was something wrong with being half-black and half-white? Did I look weird to other kids? Did I act and talk weird?* I then felt a knot come to my stomach as I stared up in the darkness toward the ceiling. *Did God think of me as half-black and half-white? Was I as special to Him as other kids?* I felt tears rolling down both sides of my face. I felt scared—maybe God didn't love me as much as other kids.

In spite of how hard I tried to go to sleep, I couldn't. Everything had now changed. I was no longer a little girl; I was a little half-black and half-white one. I turned over on my side trying not to think about it anymore but I couldn't stop. It seemed my mind wanted to recall things I'd never given much thought to before. The more questions that ran through my mind, the more I wanted to go to Mom's room and talk to her about them. But knew I couldn't—I had to be the one to answer them.

2 : BECOMING AWARE

Lying in bed, I thought back to the time when I was five and Mom put me in Montessori School. I really liked it, but I missed my mom. I wasn't used to being away from her all day. It was during my time at the Montessori School that I started to notice that my mom's color was different from the other Montessori moms' color. As I watched other kids' moms come and go, I remember knowing my mom the minute she came in the door. That was when I saw there was a color difference. Their moms were pink and mine was brown. Even then I didn't think much about it or see that it mattered. It just didn't seem important, probably because Mom had not made a big deal of it. I love my mom and she was just Mom.

Then on the day when the moms came to our school for a program, the teacher had us line up before going to sit with them. She asked each of us if we could see our mommy.

I smiled proudly, pointed to my mom and said, "That's my brown mommy."

The teacher laughed and said, "What did you say?"

I said it again with the same happy look. "That's my brown mommy!"

She laughed even harder and then called another teacher over and said, "Taniyah, tell her what you just told me. It is so cute."

The other kids were looking at me and some even started laughing. I felt confused, as if I was saying something wrong, so I would not say it again. When she said we could go sit with our moms, I rushed right over and gave my mom a big hug as I looked at the teacher.

• • •

Later that year my mom went to Washington, D. C. to help start a pilot program for inner city youth called

Champion By Choice. We stayed with columnist Jack Anderson and his family in Bethesda, Maryland. His grand-children were there and I had fun playing with them while Mom worked on plans for the program.

Then one day Mom said she wanted me to spend a day at one of the inner city elementary schools. I was excited to go to school, but when we got there I didn't want to get out of the car.

"What's wrong, honey?" Mom asked.

"Mommy, they're all brown!" I said. I was really scared. I didn't see any kids like the ones in Utah.

Mike Farley, Mr. Anderson's nephew who was in charge of the program Mom was working on, was with us. "Is she afraid of these children because they're black?" he asked.

"I think so," my mom said.

He started laughing. "Mary, I can't believe it! Your own daughter is a racist."

Mom looked at me with a real hurt look in her eyes. "Tai," she said, "these people are the same color your mom is. Are you afraid of me?"

"No, Mommy," I said. "You're my mommy."

"Then why are you afraid of them?" she asked. I couldn't answer her. I just remember feeling frightened. I had never seen so many brown people before.

"What are you teaching her?" Mike asked Mom. He was really surprised and amused by what was going on. Mike

hugged me and assured me everything would be okay.

"I guess I have never considered how sheltered my own daughter has been," Mom said sadly. "I didn't realize that she didn't know her mother is not the only brown person in the world. I just naturally assumed it didn't matter; that she would be comfortable being around my race because of me."

I didn't want Mom to feel sad, so I reached up and took her hand and smiled. "I'm not scared, Mommy," I said, although I really was.

I think Mom knew I was scared once we got inside. The classroom she left me in had all brown children, but the teacher was white.

All the children in the classroom kept staring at me. The teacher must have noticed that I was scared because she said, "I would love to have you sit right by me." She moved a desk for me next to hers. I wasn't scared anymore.

• • •

As the day passed, I decided I liked being there. I didn't like the way all the kids kept asking me if the teacher was my mother. I would laugh and say, "No, my mommy is brown." I also laughed because they didn't know brown meant their color. They started guessing what race my mom was.

"Oh, is she Spanish?" one boy asked.

Then a girl who acted as if she knew everything said, "No, stupid, she's Chinese! Can't you see she looks Chinese?"

I didn't even know I looked Chinese, but he said, "Oh yeah, she is." I was glad when the teacher told them to go sit down.

At the end of the day when my mom came for me, one of the kids came up to me and said, "If that's your mom, then is *that* your dad?" he asked, pointing with a frown on his face at Mike. Mom and Mike were busy talking to the teacher.

"No, that's Mike. He's working with my mom," I said.

"So is your dad white or what?" he asked.

I had never thought about what color my dad was so I didn't answer him.

"Well, what color *is* he?" he asked, as if he were becoming angry.

"He's pink," I said, but I thought his question was dumb. My dad was Dad and I had never thought of him as anything else.

"There are no *pink* people," he said. "You must mean white. No wonder you look *white*," he said. I didn't like the way he said that either. He made it sound as if something was wrong with how I looked.

"Well, no wonder you look *brown*," I said back to him

just the way he had said his to me. We then just stood there looking at each other. He finally said bye and left. I didn't say bye to him because he said, 'Bye, little white girl," as he laughed and walked off.

When he got to the door he called a couple of other kids over, said something to them, and pointed at me. They all started laughing. I wanted to stick my tongue out at them but knew better; Mom had told me never to do mean things unless I thought God would do it. So I smiled and waved bye. They stopped laughing for a second and looked at each other and then at me. They then started laughing again. I kept smiling until I couldn't see them anymore.

I later told Mom about the kids not knowing that they were brown and how they had started guessing what color she was after I had already told them she was brown. I also told her about the mean little boy and what he had said. She hugged me and told me it was okay; that the little boy was probably just trying to impress me. She said we would talk about it later.

• • •

On the plane home we talked about the children at the school in Washington, D.C.

"Mom, why were there so many of them and none of them looked like the kids at my school in St. George?" I asked.

She explained how some areas had large populations of Blacks and some only a few.

"Why don't we have more brown people like them in St. George?" I asked.

I listened as she described why people lived where they did. She talked about jobs and family and friends. She said all these things could play an important part in why people lived where they did.

I told her I was sorry for being afraid of brown people. She then explained to me that brown people were not referred to as brown. I sat listening intently as she talked about names and their origins. She also told me she understood how I felt being surrounded by the kids at the school. She told me how it had been for her when she first left home. She grew up with black people and then went to college where there were only Whites.

"I was much older than you, and I *had* been around Whites, yet it was extremely difficult for me to be completely surrounded by them. I wanted to go back home to the secure feeling of my family and other Blacks. So, Tai, it's understandable that you felt scared going from St. George, with a population that's ninety-nine percent white, to a school that was one hundred percent black."

"No, Mommy, the teacher was white," I said.

"Yes, I noticed," she said. "I also noticed she was the *only* one you hung around."

"Well," I said, "she was the only one who looked like the people in St. George."

"I know, honey, but when you go to an amusement park, do you pick the carousel because it's what you are used to or do you try other rides?"

"I love trying new rides, Mommy!" I said excitedly.

"Well, you must have a similar attitude when it comes to people," she continued. "Be excited about meeting new kids that you don't know. Be grateful that you have a chance to be exposed to kids who are not just white. The world isn't like St. George. There are other places with people of many different colors. Meeting someone of a different color provides a chance to learn. Okay?"

"Okay, Mommy," I said.

Mom gave me a hug. She told me she was still proud of me for being brave enough to stay at that school all day with the black children. Mom smiled and started reading.

I looked around to see if other children were on the plane. There was a little boy two seats across from me. I looked at him and smiled. He looked at me but didn't smile back.

"Mom," I whispered in her ear, "that little boy is Chinese or Japanese over there. Should I talk to him and tell him I want to get to know other people?"

Mom laughed and hugged me as she continued reading a magazine. But I was serious, so I held up my coloring book and crayons and asked if he wanted to color with me. He just sat there looking at me. His mother said something but I couldn't understand her.

As she spoke she kept smiling and nodding her head yes. She pushed the little boy's hands toward my crayons as if telling him to take them. He did. In a little while we were laughing and coloring. We had fun even though he did not speak English.

• • •

I looked at the clock and knew I'd better get to sleep. Rolling over on my other side, I tried to stop thinking and go to sleep. I knew Mom would be upset with me for staying awake so long. But then thoughts of my dad and whether he was aware that I was *different* made me feel fully awake and ready to think some more.

3 : DAD

I smiled warmly to myself as I thought about Dad and how much I loved him. Thoughts about him made me remember something he had written to me right after I was born. I eased out of bed and turned on the night light that I had recently told Mom I was too old for. Taking the album—filled with baby pictures, letters, cards, and even a strand of my hair—from my bookshelf, I sat on the floor near the light. I quietly leafed through the tons of pictures my mom had in it until I found Dad's letter. I read it slowly.

Dear Taniyah,
You came into the world two days ago. You chose
us to come to. I want you to know that we are thrilled
to death to have you. You are a beautiful little girl
with no problems or defects.
Your mother can tell you that I truly wanted a girl
—so you are a dream come true. I love you a lot and
will do whatever I can to be a good dad.
I Love You,
Dad

I wiped at the tears as I held Dad's letter close to my
heart. He did love me. It didn't matter to him that I was a
half-white and half-black little girl. I was his dream come
true.

Hearing a noise in the hall, I quickly closed the album
and jumped into the bed. I turned toward the wall so if my
mom came in, she would not see my face; I was afraid she
would see my tears.

Within a few seconds I heard my door being opened. My
heart started beating fast; I had left the album on the floor
and the night light on.

I then heard Mom say, "My goodness, I wonder why this
is on the floor?"

I did not move a muscle.

"My, my," she said. "someone *even* turned the night

light on. Oh well, guess I'll leave it on." She then quietly closed the door and left.

I rolled over and smiled. I knew I had not fooled Mom into thinking I was asleep.

I eased back out of bed and picked up the album, feeling reassured that my dad loved me, in spite of my color. I knelt by my bed with my arms folded securely around the album and thanked God for my parents and all they had done to make my being a half-black/half-white kid unimportant in their love for me; that I was their precious little girl whom they both loved dearly.

I then put the album away and got back into bed, but *not* before I turned that night light off.

4 : MOM

After getting back in bed, I thought I heard footsteps leaving my door. Mom, apparently, had been standing in the hall. I knew I had to get to sleep or she would ground me because I had not gotten a "proper" night's rest. I smiled, thinking how she would probably look tired too. I felt certain she was still trying to figure out what I had been asked. After all, she had found my night light on *and* the album on the floor.

I rolled over on my stomach and thought about how

much I loved and admired my mom. She was responsible for how my life had been shaped so far. I was always observing her as I tried becoming my own person. I often imitated her in things she did and said.

I felt my heart starting to pound as I recalled the way kids at school would stared at my mom whenever she came inside to get me. *Did they do it because she was black?* I then thought about how I had stared at the kids in Washington D.C. and tried to understand. They were not used to seeing someone black. I wondered if they were afraid of my mom because of her color as I had been of the kids in Washington, D.C.? The thought of anyone being afraid of my mom because of her color made me sad. *I should take pictures of my mom and put them up all over the school so kids can get used to seeing someone black*, I thought. I chuckled at the thought as I then tried to think about something else. However, my thoughts would not leave my mom. I wondered if she felt hurt or upset when the kids stared at her.

I couldn't recall her ever getting upset except when people would comment on what a pretty little girl I was and then ask my mom *who* I belonged to. Once, when she was lecturing, someone asked her about me. The man said he was wondering whether or not that was her daughter up on the stand with her.

"I noticed she's awful light. Is her father, your husband,

white?" he'd asked.

Mom had turned and looked at me with a real serious look on her face and then back at the man. "She is my daughter, but I hadn't noticed how light she is. I'll have to ask my husband if he's white." People started laughing and so did I, though I still did not understand that the man was saying I was *different*.

• • •

I pulled my pillow close to my heart and let the warm love I was feeling for my mom flow through me. I truly did admire her for being herself. She isn't afraid of standing alone when it comes to doing what she thinks is right. She often says to me that friends are great to have but not if you must give up honesty and what you believe for friendship. She also tells me not to fear being someone's friend simply because others might not like him. She tells me to put myself in that person's position and ask myself how I would feel. I know my values are because of her. She treats people as people. Maybe color isn't important to me because it isn't important to her. She looks more at the person.

Feeling completely awake and alert, I got back out of bed, turned on the night light, and took down the album again. I searched through it until I found a poem I had written about my mom while she was in law school. I had entered it in a local writing contest being held as a tribute to mothers. I had submitted it without my mom knowing. One evening we were going home and the radio announcer said I won grand prize in the contest. My mom nearly hit a car as she turned to ask me what contest I had entered. The man played a recording of me reading my poem about my mom. They played it for weeks.

I now stared down at it and smiled as I read it.

I Love My Mother Because…

In giving me birth
She gave me a chance to come to earth.
Though busy as a bee,
she always *has time for me.*

Although we don't always see eye to eye,
she is my model, that's no lie.
Each day I know she cares,
for when I need her, she is always *there.*
We have gotten through good times and bad
Even when she divorced my dad.
She has taught me many things,
For a mother, she is quite supreme.
This little poem I now must end
Mom does not let me stay up 'til ten.

One last thought before I go,
It is God above who blessed me so.

Mom had cried when she heard me reading it. Mom cries when she's happy! I felt proud that it made her so happy. She kept saying, "How did you do that? How did you formulate your thoughts so beautifully?" I told her I just wrote what my heart felt about her.

I closed the album and sat there knowing I had the best mom in the world. I felt the tears coming to my eyes as I thought about how hard she worked to make my world a happy one. My tears continued to fall as I recalled how much she did for me, especially when she's worked all day and then comes home to start another full time job: taking care of me. Yet she had never made me feel as if I was a pain to her. She had made two commitments to herself, and to God, if I was blessed to make it to this earth: One, she would raise me righteously; and two, she would not allow the things of this world (her career, home chores, etc.) take time and priority over her love and devotion to me.

A gentle knock on the door told me I had been caught. Mom opened the door and peeped in.

"Is everything okay, honey?" she asked.

I nodded my head not looking at her. I didn't want her to see my tears. She stood there for a few seconds, not saying anything and neither did I.

"Well, I think you'd best be getting to sleep, don't you?" she inquired softly.

I nodded again. She then leaned over, kissed me, and left, but not before she wiped the tears from my eyes. This made me cry all the more. She was really trying to understand my need to find an answer for myself even though I knew it was hurting her deeply not to be able to help. I asked God to help her know that I was all right. I never wanted my mom to be sad because of me. I felt a very warm feeling inside and thanked God.

"Thank you for my mom," I said as I tried again to fall asleep. But now God stayed heavily on my mind.

5: AM I GOD'S WILL?

Unable to sleep with thoughts of God running through my mind, I finally stood on my bed and stared out my window at the sky. It was filled with stars and I felt warm and loved as I stared up at them. I had always told Mom that the stars were angels God had watching over me. I smiled as I marveled at how many there were tonight. I felt special seeing so many of them.

I knew there was a God. My parents and grandparents, especially my mom and my nana, Marylyn Eyer, had made

Him the center of my life.

I thought back to when I was very small and how Mom would have me kneel with her to pray and how warm and special I always felt each time I did. Even though I didn't know what I was saying, I would try to imitate Mom and give the prayer.

Mom always read the scriptures to me when I couldn't read. I still remember sitting and watching her read and wanting to do it as well. Many times she would find me with the scriptures in my hand, pointing to the words and acting as if I was reading though I didn't know how. I was simply repeating some of the words I had heard her say when she read.

Both my mom and my nana had taught me to be an unselfish giver. I had never been allowed to give away things just because I no longer had any use for them. They taught me that it's a greater joy if the sacrifice means something. I had learned to give up those things that sometimes meant the most to me.

They also taught me not to be afraid to stand up for what is right and to be willing to admit when I am wrong. And most of all, to remember that God loved me and to have faith in Him.

I yawned but did not want to go lie down. Instead, I continued looking out at the stars as I thought about Mom telling me how the doctors had given up on my making it to this earth when she went into labor when she was only five months pregnant with me. She said she had just laid in bed and cried for a long time. She finally felt she should pray.

She went into the hospital bathroom so she could quietly pray without interruption. She said she began pleading with God to let me make it to this earth. While praying, she said she got the strongest feeling that she needed to pray and want the "Lord's will, not hers" to be done. She said it was difficult to want the Lord's will to be done when she wanted me so badly, yet she also understood that God knew best for her.

I closed my eyes and was about to pray when the words of a song I had learned came to mind:

> *"Heavenly Father, are you really there? Do you hear and answer a child's prayer? Some say that heaven is far away, but I feel it close around me as I pray.*
>
> *Heavenly Father, I remember now, something that Jesus told disciples long ago; 'Suffer the children to come to me.' Father, in prayer I'm coming now to thee."*
> (LDS Hymn, "A Child's Prayer")

Opening my eyes, I looked back out at the stars; a moon was now glowing softly among them: God's face. "Am I your will? Do you recognize me as your child too?" I whispered quietly.

For the longest moment the stillness of the night brought only silence between the Lord and me; a silence broken only by a tear that rolled down my face and hit the base board of the window as I remembered the miracle of my birth. In spite of the doctors saying I would never make it to this earth, I had!

I closed my eyes and smiled. I was here because it was the *Lord's* will. I felt happy inside as I thought about how I had never doubted nor questioned Mom or my nana about God and the things He wanted me to do. I now knew why— I saw God as my *friend*.

"I do believe you love me," I whispered quietly toward the sky, "even though I am half-black and half-white."

I opened my eyes and again stared at the sky. The stars and the moon were now blurry with clouds and tears of love and joy for me.

> *I am like a star shining brightly*
> *Smiling for the whole world to see.*
> *I can do and say happy things each day,.*
> *For I know Heavenly Father loves me.*
>
> (LDS Hymn)

6 : ADJUSTING

I felt myself getting tired and laid back down. I felt proud of my family for how they had helped me believe in God and in myself. I smiled and hugged my pillow as I thought of how lucky I was. I didn't want to ever disappoint them. I closed my eyes tightly and said "Oh no" as I thought about a time I had done something wrong. Having always been taught to love and treat people as I'd like to be treated, I had tried to do that but once I failed.

It had happened when I was in first grade and a boy in

my class kept calling me a black bat. I finally called him a white duck. I went home and told Mom what had happened, that I was sorry for calling him that name. I told her I got so upset that I just couldn't take it anymore.

Mom doesn't go for name calling or racism. The next day she went to school with me and requested a conference with the boy's parents. The teacher asked if there was a problem and Mom told her what had happened.

The teacher was surprised and said I should have told her about the problem. She asked Mom if she'd like to speak to the boy. My mom said yes, and the four of us (my teacher, my mom, the boy, and I) stepped outside the classroom to talk.

Mom asked him if he knew what a bat was. He told her it was an animal. She asked him what I was.

He laughed and said, "A girl."

Mom smiled and asked him if I was an animal or a human.

"Human," he said with a smile.

She asked him why he had called me a black bat.

He frowned and looked at her as if he was confused by the question. "Because she has black hair," he said.

Mom was speechless for a moment. She then pointed to herself and asked him what she was.

"A black bat," he said.

Mom looked at the teacher, who also had dark hair, and

asked what she was.

He looked at her, shrugged his shoulders and again said, "A black bat."

Mom explained to him that none of us were animals even if we did have dark hair. She also told him that calling me a black bat hurt my feelings and she did not want her daughter being referred to as a bat or any other kind of animal.

He smiled and said, "Okay."

She thanked the teacher and was about to leave when the boy said, "Will you tell her not to call me a white duck anymore?"

Mom told him I wouldn't—and I haven't.

• • •

My eyes were starting to feel heavy and I yawned again, certain that I was getting close to falling asleep, but then I found myself thinking about what I had once heard a lady ask my mom. She had wanted to know how I was adjusting, being both black and white. I didn't understand what she meant and I wanted to tell her I wasn't adjusting to being black and white, I was adjusting to being a child in what to me was a grown-ups world. Adults have lots of rules about TV, playtime, sweets, talking on the phone, studying, and all the other things you can and can't do when you're a kid.

Trying hard to fall asleep, I wondered if I was suppose to adjust to being half-black and half-white. *If so, how was I to adjust? Exactly what was I to do that would show that I was "adjusting" and to whom?* At school I didn't feel I had to adjust. The kids hadn't bothered me about being half-black and half-white. They were not rude, nor did they leave me out of things or not play with me because of my color. Only once did I wonder why a remark had been made to me and not the other kids.

A girl at school got angry when my team beat hers in a kickball game. She looked at me and yelled, "Well, at least I'm not half-black and half-white."

Everyone was quiet as they looked at me. I had felt sorry for her but all I could say was, "Well, don't blame me. It's not my fault you're not."

Recalling that incident made me now realize she probably meant it in a negative way *and* that she was very much aware that I was half-black and half-white. Also, I now understood why all the kids had become quiet; they knew it was meant to be mean and hurtful.

"Thank you, God, for not letting me know she was trying to hurt me. I probably would have cried in front of all my friends," I whispered softly as I rolled on my side.

I still felt the grown ups were the ones making race a big deal. They spent more time thinking about it than I did.

They were the ones who couldn't *adjust*.

• • •

The last thought to cross my mind before I fell asleep was how happy I was that my family had taught me about God and how important it is to have a good attitude about myself and things that happen in life. I fell asleep knowing that because of my parents and God's love, I would overcome hard times I might now face as a half-black and half-white kid. I also knew that if the day ever came when kids, or grown ups, said cruel things to hurt my feelings, perhaps even make me cry, I would never let them make me feel ashamed of my color. I was going to be just as happy being me as any other kid.

7 : WHAT RACE AM I?

As I dressed for school the next morning and looked in the mirror, the boy's question came back to my mind. If I was half-Black and half-White, then what race did I belong to? The little boy in Washington, D.C. had called me a little White girl. His words had no meaning to me then. It had been more the tone of his voice. I love both my parents and I would not choose to be one race over the other.

It was then that I remembered a conversation I had overheard my mom having with a lady who had come to our house to do a census report. I had only been five or six.

"How many are in your home?" the lady asked my mom. My mom said two and then quickly added, "and one dog."

The lady ignored the "and one dog" and said, "Both African or black American?"

My mom said, "No, my daughter is biracial."

The lady replied, "Well, that counts as being African-American."

"I'm afraid you're wrong," my mom said, sounding somewhat angry. "You don't tell me what race my child is nor will that piece of paper define for me or my daughter what race she is or place her in one category over the other. She is part of me and her dad. She will not be denied her full racial makeup by anyone. If they don't have a space on there to acknowledge or count biracial people then you best create one or don't count her at all."

"Well," the lady said, "they do have a blank on here for *Other* races, so maybe that's what it is for. I suppose I could put biracial there and in brackets write both races."

"That would be acceptable," my mom said in a very final tone of voice.

Not long after that the school needed a count of the number of students and their race. The teacher explained to us why it had to be done. We had continued our work until the lady came.

The lady who came to my class went down the different

race names and counted the students as they raised their hand for that race. Finally she said, "Now, did I count everyone?" I raised my hand.

"You didn't call out my race, so I haven't been counted," I said.

"Oh," she said, looking rather confused. "I didn't call your race?"

I shook my head.

"Well," she said looking at the paper in her hand, "I had to have called it. Were you listening?"

I nodded my head.

"Uh, well, what race are you?" she asked, still looking confused.

"Biracial," I replied. I started feeling nervous because the classroom had become so quiet. I started feeling that I shouldn't have said anything. Then I thought about my mom telling me to be proud of who I was, so I fought the fear.

"Oh, then you should have raised your hand when I said African-American," she said, looking relieved.

"But I'm not just African-American. I'm my daddy's daughter too. I am also part white."

"Yes, but we still count you as African-American," she said as if that was final.

"No, we don't," I persisted. "Unless you have permission from my daddy that his blood doesn't count you can't count me as African-American. I know my daddy; he loves me and would not want his part forgotten. I'm definitely the race that's called *biracial*." I sat looking at her with my arms folded, feeling hurt and angry that she wanted me to forget one of my parents in order to be counted.

The boy next to me had smiled and said, "All right, Taniyah," and put out his hand to give me five. It really made me feel good when he said that because I didn't know what my classmates were thinking. He said it loud enough for the lady to hear because she looked at him and then at the teacher. The teacher gave a shrug as if to say "Beats me."

I didn't know what I would do or say if she insisted on not counting me as biracial. I hadn't thought that far ahead. She looked at her sheet.

"Well, I see," she said, sounding a bit frustrated. "I guess we can write *biracial* by the word *other*."

"Thank you," I said, smiling.

"Well, thank you," she said with a smile too.

• • •

I smiled happily at myself in the mirror. I had been standing up for myself as a half-black and half-white kid even when I didn't know I was doing it. I now understood what my mom meant when having that conversation with the census taker. I couldn't accept one color and reject the other. I was who I was and I had to remember that whether I was with black or white people.

I had just twirled around happily when my mom stepped into my room.

"My, my, the little night owl is in a good mood. Care to tell your mom why?" she asked, smiling.

"I am half-black and half-white," I said cheerfully as I gave her a big hug. "And that makes me *very* happy."

"Is that what the little boy asked you, what race you were? Mom asked.

"Nope, I asked myself that question," I said. "He asked me something else. But if it will help you not to worry, it did concern my color."

"Care to tell me now?" Mom asked, with a hopeful look on her face.

"Um," I said with a grin on my face, "maybe, but only if we can go out to steak dinner tonight."

"What?" Mom said, acting shocked. I laughed.

"Just kidding, Mom," I said. "Steaks at home will be just as great!"

I rushed from the room with her chasing me and laughing as she accused me of trying to crossmail her. In the car, I told her I would tell her everything after school. I still wanted to give the boy my answer without feeling she had influenced what I would say. She said she understood.

8: IT'S TOUGH

I waited until the end of the school day to see if the boy would remember that I was to give him an answer to his question today. He did. I was glad that he remembered, I had spent a lot of time thinking about his question. I would have been a little upset if he'd forgotten to ask for my answer. However, other than a loss of sleep, seeking an answer to his question had helped me. It had helped me know myself better.

He stopped me as I was leaving. "So, Taniyah, do you know?" he asked.

I noticed he didn't even look or sound nervous.

"Know what?" I said, testing him to see if he remembered what he had asked me.

"If it's hard being half-black and half-white?" he said with a look of disappointment.

"Well, I'll answer your question if you will first answer one for me." I said.

"Sure, what's your question?" he asked.

"Why did you ask me if it was hard?" I quizzed him with a frown on my face.

"I don't know. I guess because I heard my aunt talking about her daughter marrying a black guy. She said they are going to have lots of problems. She said their children are going to face problems too because of their *stupid* decision to get married. She said it's bound to end in divorce," he explained.

"When I heard her say that, I thought about you. I told her I didn't agree because there was a girl in my class who was half-black and half-white and she was always happy. She then said that she bet you were not happy and if you had *your* way, you would not be a half-black and half-white kid. So I decided to find out if that's true. Then I can tell her if she was right or not."

He stood looking at me.

I didn't say anything. I was glad though that I had thought about it.

"Well," he said, "tell me."

"Well, it is kind of hard being a biracial kid, and that's what I am: biracial," I said proudly. "It's hard mainly because people insist on making it so. I'm happy being half-black and half-white. I wouldn't change that even if I could. I see nothing wrong with the color of my mom's skin, or my dad's, that would make me not want to be the color I am. I don't wish I was white when I see white kids, and I don't wish I was black when I see black kids. I am just proud and happy that I am the color I am.

"It would make me sad if I couldn't have both my parents color; I love both of them. I think grown ups are the ones who see kids as black or white. They have decided which color is best or at least better than the other. Now they want us to think and feel like them. But Mom says anyone with an ounce of intelligence knows that skin color does not make one person smarter nor better than another person. Do you think I am not as smart or not as good as you because I am half-black?"

"Heck no. You're much smarter than me. And I don't think I'm better than you because I am white. What have I done to be better than you?" he asked.

"I guess you don't have to do anything except be white," I answered.

"Well, that's dumb," he said.

I shrugged my shoulders. "I know. But that's how the grown-ups want it to be. Your aunt seems to feel that way. She

seems to be only seeing that guy's color. If her daughter married someone of the same color there could still be a divorce. You know white people who have gotten divorced, don't you?" I asked him.

"Yeah," he said. "My aunt is divorced and she married someone white."

"Again, I think it's grown-ups who don't want people to be together and they use skin color as an excuse. True, my parents ended up getting a divorce, but not because of color. Mom says it's not a person's color that makes a happy marriage or causes a divorce. People are human no matter what the skin color."

"I wish you could tell my aunt this neat stuff."

"Well, it probably wouldn't matter if I did. She most likely already has her mind set on believing what she wants to believe. But the next time she talks about all the problems the children will have, ask her if she's going to be one of the problems or one of the people loving them for who they are and not hating them because of their dad's color. Suggest that her love might be enough to help them overcome the problems they might have. I know my grandmas and other family members love me. Their love would be enough even if the world hated me. *They* are the people who bring true meaning to my life."

He didn't say anything.

"Furthermore," I continued, "if it's ever hard being a

biracial kid, it's because I care too much about what other people think rather than what God thinks."

"I just thought of something, Taniyah," he said. "You're right."

"What made you realize that?" I asked.

"You said people don't pick each other because of color and don't get a divorce because of color. You are dead right," he said, getting all excited. "Look at us kids. We don't pick a kid to be our friend because of color. There are things about the kid we like, right?"

"Yeah."

"And sometimes we get angry at each other. Sometimes we even stop being friends, but it isn't because of the kid's color. Right?"

"Right!" I said. "There are other reasons that things go wrong that have nothing to do with color."

"Yeah," he said.

We both laughed and gave each other five.

"Why do grown ups always want to blame everything on color?" he asked.

"Beats me," I said. "Maybe they use color as…" I searched for a good word, "well, it's a good…"

"Crutch," he said.

"Yeah, that's the word I was trying to think of," I said.

"Do you wonder why it's so easy for us to see these things while grown-ups can't?" he asked.

"Probably because we're kids. We don't have all the prejudging,—I mean prejudice—they have. Plus, we're smart enough to talk about this stuff."

"Yeah, you're right. My aunt should talk to her daughter's boyfriend and let him know how she feels."

"She's probably afraid to. Mom says a lot of prejudice is based on fear. Were you scared to ask me if it was hard being a biracial kid?"

"Yeah! Well, sort of. I was afraid you would think it was a dumb question and get all mad—I mean *angry*—at me," he admitted, smiling.

"Why?"

"I don't know."

"If others had said that biracial kids were mean and loved to fight, would you have asked me that question?

"Heck no."

"Why not?"

"I wouldn't want to get beat up."

"Is it fair to think that about me?" I asked as I stared at him.

"No," he said.

"Why?"

"Because you're nice." He paused. "Oh, I see what you are saying. How would kids know that *all* biracial kids were mean?" he said smiling. "They wouldn't, would they?"

"*I don't think so,*" I said, imitating Macaulay Culkin. We started laughing as we gave each other five again.

"Man, I can't wait to talk to my aunt," he said.

"Good luck," I said. "Grown ups always want us to listen to them, but they rarely, if ever, listen to us."

"I know she'll probably think I'm dumb," he said. "She'll probably say, 'You're only a kid, what do you know?' But I have to try, right?"

"I guess so," I replied. "If you don't try, you'll never know if she would have had a change of heart. Well, I've gotta be going. My mom is quite worried about how quiet I was last night. See ya."

"Thanks, Taniyah. See ya tomorrow."

"Okay," I said and turned to go meet Mom.

She was leaning over, looking intently in my direction. I smiled thinking she had identified the questioner and was now awaiting the details. I decided I would pretend I couldn't remember a thing and maybe she would suggest going out for a steak dinner to help jog my memory.

• • •

That night Mom listened intently during dinner (*spaghetti*, at home) as I told her about the boy's question and the talk he and I had after school. I told Mom I felt my world would never be as it once was and deep inside I felt scared. She did not say anything right away, instead, she sat staring at the table. Smiling, she finally looked at me and started humming a song (Mom has long given up on trying to sing; *thank goodness!*). Smiling too, I began singing the words she was humming:

> *"God has numbered in the sky, all the stars that shine on high. Worlds so great and sparrows small; God is watching over all.*
>
> *He remembers night and day, every child at work or play. He will teach you what to do; God is watching over* you."
>
> (LDS Hymn, "God Is Watching Over All")

• • •

Later that evening Mom and I went for a walk. All around the neighborhood were signs of Christmas, from glowing Christmas lights to music flowing from different homes. The world seemed so peaceful and full of love and harmony, but Mom knew (and I now knew) that this feeling would exist only for a small moment and that my world would not go unchallenged; there would be many who would have nothing better to do than to seek to create *conditional* love among people.

As we walked and talked, I understood, as best I could, how important it was going to be for me to be strong and to hold on to the Lord's hand.

• • •

I stood staring out my window long after Mom thought I was asleep; my heart was so full of thoughts of the Savior and Heavenly Father until sleep just would not come.

How could the Father tell the world of love and tenderness? He sent His Son, a newborn babe, with peace and holiness.

How could the Father show the world the pathway we should go? He sent His Son to walk with men on earth, that we may know.

How could the Father tell the world of sacrifice, of death? He sent His Son to die for us and rise with living breath.

What does the Father ask of us? What do the scriptures say? Have faith, have hope, live like His Son, help others on their way.

What does he ask? Live like His Son.

(LDS Hymn, "He Sent His Son")

"Thank you, Heavenly Father," I whispered. "I will try always to trust in you with all my heart, knowing that you can and will see me through whatever difficult times lie ahead. Good night."